Street Bikes

Jesse Young

Reading consultant:
John Manning, Professor of Reading
University of Minnesota

Capstone Press
MINNEAPOLIS

C A P S T O N E   P R E S S

2440 Fernbrook Lane • Minneapolis, Minnesota 55447

Printed in the United States of America.

Library of Congress Cataloging-in-Publication Data
Young, Jesse, 1941-
    Street bikes / by Jesse Young.
    p. cm.
    Includes bibliographical references and index.
    ISBN 1-56065-227-6
    1. Motorcycles--Juvenile literature. [1. Motorcycles] I. Title. II. Series.
TL440.15.Y68 1995
796.7'5--dc20

                                    94-22828
                                      CIP
                                       AC

ISBN: 1-56065-227-6

99 98 97 96   8 7 6 5 4 3 2

Table of Contents

Chapter 1

The Road With the Most Curves

People ride street bikes for many reasons. Street biking is a cheap and fast way to get around town. It is also a great way to enjoy the passing scenery.

A street biker may take a three-hour ride along a river road, or a week-long camping trip across the country. He or she can wind up and down curving mountain roads or make a flat-out run across the desert at night. Yet street bikes also are a practical means of everyday transportation.

The Honda Gold Wing offers a scenic—and comfortable—ride.

Most riders say that street bikes let you see, hear, and feel the scenery as it flies by. Riding in a car just isn't the same. Eventually, most street bikers stop looking for the fastest way to their destination. Instead, they look for the most scenic ride.

Chapter 2

A Look at Motorcycling

Motorcycles were first made popular through racing. Races of the early 1900s were thrilling contests of speed, skill, and danger. By the 1920s, the British were building the best single-cylinder, **four-stroke** motorcycles. This was the Golden Era of Motorcycles.

During the **Depression** of the 1930s, many people rode motorcycles. It was a cheap way to travel, and it worked for basic transportation and for business trips. Motorcycles even came in handy for **bootleggers** during **Prohibition**.

   As racing drew bigger crowds, Germans and
Italians also began making good motorcycles.
In 1939, the German BMW motorcycle led the
world in competitive racing.
   After World War II (1939-1945), people in
the United States wanted the most famous
motorcycles—British Nortons and Triumphs.
These machines were very popular at the first
major motorcycle race in the United States at
Daytona Beach, Florida, in 1949.

The first great American-made motorcycle was the Harley-Davidson WLA45. During World War II, 90,000 of them were built for U.S. and British troops. These bikes were cheap and reliable. They helped motorcycling become popular in the United States.

After World War II, companies such as Volkswagen began making inexpensive cars. People bought them and put aside their motorcycles. Manufacturers hired designers to work on automobiles, not motorcycles. There were very few improvements in motorcycle design or performance during the 1940s and 1950s.

That all changed in 1959 when the Japanese Honda motorcycle appeared at the Grand Prix (French for "big prize"). This important race, on the Isle of Man in the Irish Sea, dates back to the early 1900s.

Following its 1959 Grand Prix appearance, the Honda company won every major race in Europe for the next few years. The Japanese had started a revolution in the world of motorcycles.

Chapter 3

Types of Street Bikes

The Lightweight

Lightweight motorcycles have their beginnings in World War II. Like **paratroopers**, they were parachuted into battlefields. They were good for getting around these battlefields easily and quickly. After the war, the Vespa, a small, sporty Italian motor scooter, made motorcycling look like fun to people in the United States.

The first Honda was the famous 50 cubic-centimeter (3.4 cubic-inch) lightweight. It opened up a brand new market for motorcycles. Its small size made motorcycle riding popular for everyone. "You meet the nicest people on a Honda" said one early Honda advertisement.

A lightweight motorcycle's engine is as small as 50 cubic centimeters (3.4 cubic inches) and as large as 250 cubic centimeters (15.3 cubic inches). A 250 cubic-centimeter motorcycle is probably the world's most common bike.

But when riding long distances, it's hard to keep up your speed on a lightweight bike. **Crosswinds** and speeding trucks also make them tough to handle on the highway.

A heavier bike–500 cubic centimeters (30.5 cubic inches) and up–is best for the open road. The larger engines and heavier frames make them better for long-distance riding.

Middleweight Motorcycles

The Japanese also built the best middleweight motorcycles. In the late 1960s, they turned out several models of 500 cubic-centimeter (30.5 cubic-inch) bikes. These

Middleweight bikes are stable on the open road but easier to handle than heavy touring bikes.

bikes went faster than any similar German or British middleweights.

Early Hondas were popular, but ugly. Their square headlights and **stamped steel frames** made them look clunky. When Honda introduced the Super Hawk 305, they gave it the modern look that U.S. riders wanted. The

Super Hawk carried a reliable **electrical system**, and could accelerate to over 100 miles (161 kilometers) per hour. This new Honda also had a **tubular** frame and **telescopic front forks**.

In 1970, Honda introduced front **disc brakes** on their Honda 750. Disc brakes were a breakthrough in motorcycle design.

Early motorcycles had used mechanical **drum brakes**. These brakes were similar to early automobile brakes. Two **"shoes,"** located inside each wheel's steel drum, expanded against the drum to stop the bike.

Disc brakes use two brake pads that press against a rotating disc. This action slows the motorcycle more smoothly.

Good brakes are important on any model of street

Disc brakes give a smoother stop.

Café racers started in Europe, then spread to the United States.

bike. Most bikes that have appeared on the market since 1970 use front and rear disc brakes.

Café Racers and Choppers

In Europe during the early 1960s, some young people liked to spend their time in cafés. They would often race down roads on their motorcycles at top speed. They would try to get to the next café before the song playing on the radio was over. Their bikes were called **"café racers."**

In the United States, **"choppers"** were part of this craze. They had already arrived in the United States in the late 1950s. In the 1960s, they became the American version of the European café racer.

Chopper owners like to **customize** their bikes. Their owners cut or "chop" the frame at the steering neck above the front wheel. Then they weld the neck back on at a sharp angle.

This makes handling the bike easier on long, straight roads. But choppers have poor cornering because of the long **wheelbase**. Today, a chopper is any motorcycle with a customized front end.

Chapter 4
Superbikes

In the heavyweight class, Harley-Davidson has captured about half the market. Germany's BMW and the four big Japanese companies–Honda, Kawasaki, Suzuki, and Yamaha–share the other half. The Japanese try to win more of the big-bike market by adding features. These additions include **cruise control**, electronic **fuel monitoring**, and automatic **adjustable suspension**.

Classic Superbikes

A **superbike** is a powerful, high-performance machine. There have been many such bikes

Superbikes are faster, more powerful, and more agile than other types of street bikes.

since 1900 and the beginning of motorcycles. Certain features on the early models made them superbikes: high horsepower engines, full suspension at both the front and rear, good brakes, and quick handling.

The demand for superbikes started in the 1960s. At that time, many young adults in the U.S. had extra money to spend. They wanted to buy something that would display their new wealth and make a lot of noise.

The big British and American motorcycles were exactly what they wanted. The Triumph 650 cubic-centimeter (39.7 cubic-inch) **vertical twin** was a well-known British superbike. The vertical twin engine had **cylinders** that sat side-by-side, a design that many other companies copied.

Another British classic was the Brough Superior 980 cubic-centimeter (59.8 cubic-inch) V-twin. Its smooth performance earned this bike the nickname of "the Rolls-Royce of motorcycles."

The 850 cubic-centimeter (52 cubic-inch) Norton Commando, with a vertical twin cylinder engine, was popular in both Britain and the United States.

But the engines in these motorcycles were not as efficient as Japanese engines. The

British companies of BSA-Triumph, Norton, and Brough did not survive heavy competition with the Japanese. The American company of Harley-Davidson did.

The Japanese Bikes

In 1969, Honda released its popular CB750. Five years later, the company produced another winner called the Gold Wing. The standard Gold Wing was the GL1000, which weighed more than 500 pounds (186.6 kilograms). The fancier model was the GL1500, which weighed nearly 650 pounds (242.6 kilograms).

Kawasaki followed quickly with its Z1100GP. Honda and Kawasaki were leading the superbike race, but Suzuki and Yamaha were following closely. Suzuki's best model, the Katana GSX1100S, rode well on the race track as well as the street.

With improved aerodynamics, Yamaha and other Japanese makes quickly became the best superbikes in the world.

The Japanese companies did much to improve engine designs as well as the **aerodynamic** shapes of motorcycles. All four companies list several sizes–from 750 cubic centimeters (45.8 cubic inches) to 1500 cubic centimeters (91.5 cubic inches).

The Superbike Changes

To increase horsepower or provide better control, riders customized their superbikes with American parts. The Japanese companies noticed this trend. They made changes in their bikes to give the customers what they wanted. Honda, Yamaha, Kawasaki and Suzuki have become the "bullet bikes" of today. They can be raced with very few changes made by the customer.

Front fairings and aerodynamic shapes allow racing superbikes to cut through the wind at top speed.

Chapter 5

Riding a Motorcycle

Riding a motorcycle is easier than it used to be. The key to any street bike is handling. And the key to handling is cornering. Over the last 30 years, changes in tire design and **frame geometry** have greatly improved motorcycle cornering.

Whether you are a top-level road racer or just riding your street bike around town, you have to know cornering. You can learn something about it by watching racers. At high speeds, they must lean into the turn at a sharp angle. The sharper the turn, the farther they lean. On short turns, they go faster. The wider or longer the turn, the less they have to lean.

Most bikes–whether they are choppers, café racers, or lightweight Hondas–are judged by their handling. Many racers give up comfort and good handling if their motorcycles are fast. But for long-distance touring, motorcyclists want reliable engines, good brakes, comfort, and handling.

Lightweight bikes are easy to handle for short trips around town. Middleweights are more difficult to handle, but they can reach higher speeds. The heavyweight bikes make touring comfortable.

Some bikes have it both ways. The BMW 900 is a solid touring bike and a speedy café racer. The Kawasaki 900 is also good for both track and street.

Touring bikes such as the Kawasaki Voyager or the Honda Gold Wing weigh 1,000 pounds (373.2 kilograms) and still reach speeds of 100 miles (161 kilometers) per hour. They also

The big engines on heavyweight bikes can pull these machines down the highway for long distances.

Disc brakes are now standard equipment on front and rear wheels.

have large gas tanks. These allow the rider to travel longer distances.

The bike's design gives it added comfort. The angle and width of the front fork, the long wheelbase, and the soft suspension make the ride smooth. The owner may not care that the bike does not corner as well as a superbike.

Cruise control allows the driver to set a speed and not have to hold the **throttle**. Heavy bikes, such as the Yamaha Venture, also **track true** on the highway. The engine is mounted low in the frame, making the center of gravity low. This means that the driver does not have to wrestle to keep the bike upright.

The **shaft drive** makes touring bikes quieter. Many of these bikes also have full **fairing**, a shield that covers the front of the motorcycle. The fairing helps the bike break steadily through the air, making the ride fast and comfortable.

You can ride eight to twelve hours a day on a comfortable touring bike. It's like riding in your living room. You can adjust the handlebars to fit your height. Both the driver and passenger have backrests and armrests. There is a stereo with speakers in the front and back. Saddle bags, luggage racks, and touring packs can carry camping equipment and clothing.

There is a street bike for every purpose. There is the lightweight, single-cylinder, 50 cubic-centimeter (3.4 cubic-inch) model. There are the superbikes, with their raw power and speed, and there are the comfortable touring bikes. Each is different, but all are called street bikes. As the 21st century approaches, street bikes will probably continue to be the world's most popular motorcycles.

Glossary

adjustable suspension–allows the rider to change the amount of air pressure in the shock absorbers and front forks. This makes for a smooth or stiff ride.

aerodynamic–relating to how moving air affects an object

bootleggers–those who sell or transport alcoholic beverages illegally

café racers–motorcycles driven by French youths of the 1960s

choppers–street bikes with extra-long front forks

crosswinds–winds which blow across a road from side to side

cruise control–a device that allows the rider to maintain speed without holding open the throttle

customize–to remove and add parts according to one's taste

cylinder–the container for the piston as it moves up and down

Depression–a period of economic hardship and unemployment during the 1930s

disc brakes–a system of two brake pads which press against a rotating disc, using fluid pressure to move the pads

drum brakes–brake system where two "shoes" slow a vehicle by pressing outward against a wheel-mounted drum

electrical system–the system that provides electricity for the motorcycle's lights and ignition

fairing–a plastic shield mounted on the front of the bike with a clear screen to cut the wind and protect riders

four-stroke–an engine in which there is a power stroke (following the air intake and compression strokes) in which the spark plug ignites the gas-air mixture

frame geometry–the shape of the frame determines how the bike will handle.

fuel monitoring–a system that provides data on fuel use and available mileage based on remaining fuel

paratroopers–soldiers who parachute onto battlefields

Prohibition–the period from 1920 to 1933 when the sale of liquor was not permitted in the United States

shaft drive–the rotating shaft that transfers power from the transmission to the rear wheel

shoes–a part of the brake system that slows the wheel

stamped steel frame–a sheet metal frame formed by stamping or pressing sheet metal into shape and then welding it together to form the frame

superbike–a powerful street bike often used for racing

telescopic front forks–a shock absorbing system in which one tube slides up and down inside another

throttle–a part that is responsible for feeding fuel to the engine

track true–to adjust to the conditions of the road, allowing the bike to handle bumps, dips, and holes

tubular–tubes bent and welded to form the frame of the bike. They are stronger than stamped steel.

vertical twin–an engine configuration that sets two cylinders in a "V" shape in the motorcycle frame

wheelbase–the distance from the front to rear wheel

To Learn More

Kahaner, Ellen. *Motorcycles*. Mankato, MN: Capstone Press, 1991.

Lafferty, Peter and David Jefferis. *Superbikes: The History of Motorcycles*. New York: Franklin Watts, 1990.

Sheffer, H.R. *Cycles*. Mankato, MN: Crestwood House, 1983.

Baumann, Elwood D. *An Album of Motorcycles and Motorcycle Racing*. New York: Franklin Watts, 1982.

Stewart, Gail. *Motorcycle Racing*. Mankato, MN: Crestwood House, 1988.

You can learn more about street bikes in the following magazines: *Cycle World*, *Motorcycling*, and *Sport Rider*.

Some Useful Addresses

**Canadian Motorcycle Association/
L'Association motocycliste canadienne**
500 James St. N. #201
Hamilton, ON L8L 8C4

American Motorcyclist Association (AMA)
33 Collegeview Road
P.O. Box 6114
Westerville, OH 43081-6114

Index

Honda motorcycles, 12, 15-16, 18, 23, 34; Gold Wing, 6, 28, 34; GL1000, 28; GL1500, 28; 750, 19; Super Hawk 305, 18-19;

Isle of Man, 12

Kawasaki motorcycles, 23; Z1100GP, 28; 900, 34; Voyager, 34

Norton, 27

paratrooopers, 15
Prohibition, 9

racing, 9-10, 12, 20-21, 30

superbikes, 12, 23, 26-27, 30, 37-38
suspension, 23, 26, 37
Suzuki motorcycles, 23; Katana GSX1100S, 28, 30

touring, 16, 34, 36-38

Vespa, 15
Volkswagen, 12

World War II, 10, 12

Yamaha, 23, 28